797,885 Books
are available to read at

Forgotten Books

www.ForgottenBooks.com

Forgotten Books' App
Available for mobile, tablet & eReader

ISBN 978-1-330-05711-7
PIBN 10014946

This book is a reproduction of an important historical work. Forgotten Books uses state-of-the-art technology to digitally reconstruct the work, preserving the original format whilst repairing imperfections present in the aged copy. In rare cases, an imperfection in the original, such as a blemish or missing page, may be replicated in our edition. We do, however, repair the vast majority of imperfections successfully; any imperfections that remain are intentionally left to preserve the state of such historical works.

Forgotten Books is a registered trademark of FB &c Ltd.
Copyright © 2015 FB &c Ltd.
FB &c Ltd, Dalton House, 60 Windsor Avenue, London, SW19 2RR.
Company number 08720141. Registered in England and Wales.

For support please visit www.forgottenbooks.com

1 MONTH OF FREE READING

at

www.ForgottenBooks.com

By purchasing this book you are eligible for one month membership to ForgottenBooks.com, giving you unlimited access to our entire collection of over 700,000 titles via our web site and mobile apps.

To claim your free month visit:

www.forgottenbooks.com/free14946

* Offer is valid for 45 days from date of purchase. Terms and conditions apply.

Similar Books Are Available from
www.forgottenbooks.com

The Little Boss
A Comedy Drama in Four Acts, by Frank L. Bixby

The Ratnavali
A Sanskrit Drama, by Harṣavardhana Srīsachandra Chakravartī

A Scout's Honor
A Play for Boys in One Act, by Clifton Lisle

Shakspere's Holinshed
The Chronicle and the Historical Plays Compared, by W. G. Boswell Stone

Three Plays for Puritans
Being the Third Volume of His Collected Plays, by Bernard Shaw

Sleepy Hollow
A Romance of the Revolution in Three Acts, by George M. Rosener

A Study of the Drama
by Brander Matthews

A Treasury of Plays for Children
by Montrose Jonas Moses

Napoleon
A Play, by Herbert Trench

Mice and Men, A Romantic Comedy in Four Acts
by Madeleine Lucette Ryley

Five One Act Plays
by Stanley Houghton

Freytag's Technique of the Drama
An Exposition of Dramatic Composition and Art, by Gustav Freytag

The Importance of Being Earnest
A Trivial Comedy for Serious People, by Oscar Wilde

The Melting-Pot
Drama in Four Acts, by Israel Zangwill

The Best Plays of 1920-1921
by John Arthur Chapman

Selected Dramas of John Dryden
With the Rehearsal, by George Villiers

Six Dramas of Calderón
by Calderón De La Barca

The Chinese Drama
by William Stanton

Robespierre
A Lyrical Drama, by R. H. Patterson

The Plays of Moliere, Vol. 1
by Molière

ELFRIDA.

A DRAMA.

BY
DYSON RISHELL.

PHILADELPHIA:
J. B. LIPPINCOTT & CO.
1883.

PS2714
R6

Copyright, 1882, by J. B. LIPPINCOTT & Co.

DRAMATIS PERSONÆ.

EDGAR, King of England.
DUNSTAN, Archbishop of Canterbury.
ORDGAR, Earl of Devon, father of Elfrida.
THE EARL OF CORNWALL.
ATHELWOLD,
EDMUND,
OSRIC,
EGBERT,
} Lords attending King Edgar.
GAFNEY, a young lord, in love with Elfrida.
ROGER, attending Athelwold, in love with Roxie.
PHILIP, a servant, in love with himself.
ELFRIDA.
JUDITH, wife of Ordgar, mother of Elfrida.
ROXIE, attending Elfrida.
SANCIE, an ignorant cook.
DURK, a laughing boy.
A woman, Durk's mother.
Officers, messengers, etc.

ELFRIDA.

ELFRIDA.

ACT I.

SCENE I.—KING EDGAR'S PALACE.

Enter KING EDGAR, *the* EARL OF DEVON, *the* EARL OF CORNWALL.

KING EDGAR.

So here's a quarrel for a little glebe
No bigger than my hat,—scarce large enough
To hold the graves of those who died for it!
For shame, my lords, to vex us with your brawl
About a garden!

DEVON.

      Ten good leagues, Your Grace,
Beyond the Tamar he doth cast me out.

CORNWALL.

And every league my own.

DEVON.
               Not so!

KING EDGAR.

Wait now, and I will hear you. Ordgar, you
Being the eldest, let us hear your claim;
The other wait in silence our command.
Now we will hear you, Devon.

DEVON.

What lies beyond our ancient boundaries,
That on the south may serve at Cornwall's will,—
For of his petty leagues not one I covet;
'Tis not mine, and never was my father's,—
But on the Tamar's bank my conscience sits,
And, looking northward, doth defend my sword.
Its right is vested, and hath ever been,
In me and my forefathers, saving now
That Cornwall most unjustly claims its right.

KING EDGAR.

Now Cornwall, Devon doth demand his own,
Because of ancient, undisputed right:
What say you for yourself in your demand?

CORNWALL.

So much doth Cornwall of his right demand,—

That this fair province, which of late was got
By rude and martial arguments from him,
Be straight delivered up, his right thereto
In decent haste conceded,—holding this
Upon the ancient, just, and valid claim
That in Earl Godwin's time, now thirty years
This earl, his father, risked some old demand
Upon the rough arbitrament of war.
So was it that his father lost, and gave,
Hard pressed upon by his indignant foe,
This province as a small indemnity.
Thus having paid his debt, the son steps in
And many years did strive to get it back
Till in the chance of war he hath it now.

King Edgar.

To this, my lord, what answer wilt thou make?

Devon.

So answer we this Cornwall: He did win
Some thirty years ago a certain cause;
This, to the self-same arbiter appealed,
Hath been reversed, and thereby all his claims,
Which valid were some thirty years ago,
Are by his chosen court now set aside.

King Edgar.

My Lord of Devon, we do think you wrong,
And see no merit in the title noised
By Cornwall.   Neither being, then, in right,
Shall neither win to make an endless fight.
You did good service in my father's wars:
For this I thank you.   But I take this land
In right of my grandfather, Athelstan,
Who from the invading Welsh did wring it back.
And now we charge you, as you love our weal,
To draw your partisans away and go.

Devon.

My lord, is justice nothing, and these wars?
Four hundred years 'twas Devon past dispute;
So is it now, with all its ancient right
By later conquests stronger still confirmed.

Cornwall.

By prior conquest 'tis confirmed in me.

King Edgar.

Why, in God's name, my lords the suit is done.
I would divide it if a single line
Could run its widthless course between your parts
And leave a grave on either side to share.

DEVON.

Ten leagues beyond the Tamar from my own,—

KING EDGAR.

Enough, enough! Pray get you from our sight.
[*Exit.*

SCENE II.—THE PALACE.

KING EDGAR, DUNSTAN, ATHELWOLD, EGBERT, OSRIC,
EDMUND, ORNIM, *and* ATTENDANTS.

KING EDGAR.

Is it considered what you ask,—my right,
And symbol of that adequate command
Which bade you quit your humble abbacy
To be a dignitary, stay, and prop
Beneath itself, not topping o'er its head?
For seven years! my crown! to render up
This trinket to your whim! How old art thou?

DUNSTAN.

I've seen the backs of nine and forty years.

King Edgar.

Why, only four and thirty laggard years
Have I kicked sprawling for my very mirth.
But those which late have come are pale with fright,
And scurry by lest I should serve them so.
But now I love them better than I did,
And fain would have them tarry if they dared.
'Tis time we put these childish toys away,
Though I do love this gaud. I'll fill it up
With rattles, tinkling bells, and noisy tin,
And play at baby with you seven years.

Dunstan.

My lord grows merry; kings must have their sport,
But in this hour of solemnity,
When thou surrenderest up thy diadem
In penance for a grievous, heinous sin,
'Tis meet that reverence and humility
Befitting such occasion should prevail.
My lord, no controversy threatens you,
For none doth give the thing that he would take,
Nor vex himself with angry disputations
When rosy Truth sits smiling in his lap.
Now, as the guardian of Your Highness' soul
And chief conservator of this your state,

Which we have rescued from such adverse swords,
We charge you give this splendor to our care.

ATHELWOLD.

Is Edgar but a puppet jumped by strings,
Thou grown to we, the king a barren naught?
"We!" By my faith, lord bishop, count yourself.

DUNSTAN.

Tut, boy! Whilst thou wert blubbering at school
For spanks bought with thy rude impertinence,
I, who now speak with such authority
For virtues calling for redress to heaven,
Stood in the estimation of the world.

ATHELWOLD.

My liege, command us seize this lofty priest
Who all his proper functions hath surpassed,
Assumes a majesty that fits him ill,
And even here demands the very crown.

OSRIC.

Speak but the word, my lord, and it is done.

EDMUND.

        Down with the priest!

Egbert.

Hold, hold! Let the lord bishop speak.

Dunstan.

Pitch out these rude combustibles. Away,
Away, curst Edmund! Cast Lord Osric hence!
But touch my sacred body with your hands,
And I will open up the gates of heaven.

King Edgar.
      Peace, peace!

Dunstan.

Not now, my lords, not now, but some time hold
Yourselves in readiness to answer this.

Athelwold.

"Some time!" I would that all my enemies
Would wag their heads and bite their teeth and say,
"Some time I'll so-and-so and so-and-so."
"Some time," methinks, is but a trundle-bed
Where weaklings do their sick ambition lay,—
Where thou dost put until thou canst forget
This enterprise, too weak to help itself,
Too heavy to be carried on thy heart.

DUNSTAN.

You do mistake me, Athelwold. To-day
The king delivers up his crown to me.
The rest shall wait its season. Doubt it not.

KING EDGAR.

My lords, we let the bishop have his way:
What care we for the bauble? Let the fools
Who wish it have it. It is naught to me.

ATHELWOLD.

Farewell to majesty! A juggler sits
Beside the throne of England, and the king
Allies to work his own calamity.

KING EDGAR.

Nay, Athelwold, I do this of my will,—
Or, if it please you, from my want of it,—
And care not here nor there. Here is the crown.

DUNSTAN.

Now, noble Edgar, thou art king indeed,
With this, thy rival, held in custody.
Kneel, kneel, my lords, and say, "Long live the
    king!"

ALL (*but* ATHELWOLD).

    Long live the king!

KING EDGAR.

What, Athelwold! canst thou not wish me live?

ATHELWOLD.

Long life to Edgar! Yonder is the king.

KING EDGAR.

Ho! ho! My Lord the Bishop speaks it well.
This golden circle I resign to him,
While I am king indeed.

ATHELWOLD.

                  I wish it so.
I have no more to say. God save you all!

KING EDGAR.

What was it, Egbert, thou didst say this morn
Concerning one Elfrida? On my life,
The nun was wearisome as autumn winds
Or the interpretation of a jest.
'Twas villainous, my lords, most villainous,
In me. I thank thee, Dunstan, for thy care.
Where is Elfrida, whom you speak so fair?

Egbert.

She is the Earl of Devon's daughter, sire,
Old Ordgar, who did vex Your Highness' ear
With his loud scramble here the other day
For a small province.

King Edgar.

     Oh, I remember.
Come, Egbert; hast thou seen the maid thyself?
Come, come!
   [*Exeunt all but* Dunstan.

Dunstan.

Now give him rein, and let him choose his toys.
This circlet hath no virtue, no avail,
But 'gainst his will, in presence of the lords,
To wrench it from his brow,—that was a sign
Which hath a meaning. Ay, my royal clown,
Have thy own way, but touch not sovereignty.
       [*Exit.*

SCENE III.—THE PALACE.

King Edgar *and* Athelwold.

King Edgar.

Now, Athelwold, commend me to my lord,
And to our court at Reading summon here
The fair Elfrida, if she please your eye.
Our judgment is not thus inflexible
Where but a hair divides the right and wrong;
Then thou shalt say to Ordgar, "Have thy land."
The brightest-gleaming jewels oft are digged
From most unlikely mines; so seems it now.
This Egbert hath an eye,—methinks he hath;
But, mark you, Athelwold, he sees so well—
Now, Athelwold, such villainy's in man—
He'd take a look upon his own account.
But thou art trustier. Now, my lord, farewell.

Athelwold.

Men are stiff arguments 'gainst Providence;
Women **our** refutation, his excuse.

King Edgar.

Most excellent, most excellent they are.

And I no coward in so sweet a war
As that which women wage 'gainst lusty man
When he enlists his mettle. That you know.
Now get you back to Reading speedily.
If this new citadel be worth the siege,
And vindicate the botch of heaven in me,
So good, and let the confutation fit.
But be thou, Edgar, only with thine eyes
To note her face, her gesture, and her form,
And see if she doth carry like a queen.
For if she move uncouthly like a cow,
Or waddle like a fish-dame on the sand,
She hath such tricks will make her all unfit
To serve as England's queen in Edgar's time.

ATHELWOLD.

I know a woman when I see her, sir,
And will not send thee on a fruitless quest;
Nor fear she may elude Your Majesty
When laughing "Yes" plays peep behind her "No,"
Because, my lord, I'll have an eye to that.

KING EDGAR.

Nay, say you nothing. Get you back in haste·
I'll do the winning when she reaches me.
Another sent to woo another's love

Sets roguery afoot, and ties the hounds.
But take my eyes, and leave thyself at home.
Now haste thee to Elfrida, Athelwold,
And see how well she may confute a king.
How soon wilt thou be gone?

ATHELWOLD.

        To-morrow, sir.

KING EDGAR.

Good, very good.

SCENE IV —A FOREST IN DEVONSHIRE.

Enter ATHELWOLD.

ATHELWOLD.

I would I were a hermit dwelling here
Amidst these birches all the four-winged year,
To crush the hoar-frost, saying, This is love,
And so I crush you that hath frozen me.
Then, when the frost, which is so like to love,
Had kissed the trustful roses till they died,
I'd sing the barren earth defiant songs.

SONG.

Let the brown earth lie; what care
  Have I that 'tis sad,
That the fields are dull and bare,
  That the hills are clad
In a faded, tattered dress,
  Like a beggar's child,
Asking alms, in their distress,
  Of the snow-clouds wild?
    Oh, the earth was fair to see,
      Now 'tis grieving, dying;
    Tuneful birds, once mad with glee,
    Singing all day long for thee,
      Voiceless southward now are flying.

How you mocked me when my grief
  Haunted like a ghost!
How you flaunted every leaf
  When I sorrowed most!
Flinging every joy you had
  Toward my grieving eye!
Taunting earth, oh I am glad
  When I see you die!
    Oh, the earth was fair, etc.

Half that's reality,—enough for grief
And all the vagrant passions of the soul
To feed and fatten on. How well they thrive
Upon the bitter morsels dropping down
From off the burdened table of our joys!

ELFRIDA.
>Help! help!

ATHELWOLD.
>What's that?

It is such music as a harp that fell
Undinted from a window of sweet heaven
Might give when vexed by the rude winds of earth,
So sweet and yet so pitiful it is.

ELFRIDA.
>Help! help!

ATHELWOLD.

It is a cry for help. (*Sees her.*) Oh, saddest sight!
Is that a stain of blood upon thy cheek?
Why did the jealous seraphs cast thee forth
To fall so bruised among these cruel thorns?

ELFRIDA.

I pray you help me rise. My limbs will hold
If I do get upon my feet again.

ATHELWOLD.

Alas, alas! these human arms of mine
Are all too rude to bear a spirit up,

ELFRIDA.

    Oh, where is my palfrey?

ATHELWOLD.

Thy palfrey! Hadst thou need of palfreys there?

ELFRIDA.

Sir knight,—for such I do perceive thou art,—
I am too weak to know what thou wouldst ask.
I beg you let me sit upon this bank,
And you may bring me water from the brook.
Then, if my palfrey hath not strayed too far,
Wilt thou pursue him? for I cannot walk,
So far the castle is from here.

ATHELWOLD.

It is an angel's voice, an angel's form,
But in her weakness and her many needs
She is a woman, which is better still.
So sit you here upon this mossy bank,
The elf-queen's throne, and bid me what you will.
How came your palfrey gone?

ELFRIDA.

                  We broke away
When with my father hawking, and in sport

I urged him through these forests, calling back,
"Pray do not follow me." Here from these thorns
A wild boar rushing forth did frighten him,
And how I fell I know not, but I lay
Too weak with fright, vexation, grief, and pain
To do aught else than feebly call for help.

ATHELWOLD.

Why when I came this brook was giggling by;
The witless birds sang merrily above,
As if it were a holiday, and Pain
Had learned his duty, and not overta'en
The loveliest form he ever did pursue.

ELFRIDA.

       I beg you find my palfrey.

ATHELWOLD.

He must be near, and yet he is not here.
The idle beast, and ignorant and wild,
To stray away from so much loveliness!

ELFRIDA.

I think his tracks are printed in the clay.

ATHELWOLD.

The foolish beast, so steeped in knavery
That he could leave you!

ELFRIDA.

        Look you on the ground.

ATHELWOLD.

I did, my lady, but I saw no feet.
I think the earth was shamed to see him fly,
And would not own the grievance of his feet.

ELFRIDA.

    Sir knight, forgive me, but thy name?

ATHELWOLD.

My name is Athelwold, and from the court
Of Edgar, our good liege, I have a charge.

ELFRIDA.

    And I, Elfrida, here of Devonshire.

ATHELWOLD.

Oh, not Elfrida! Can it be thou art?
Then farewell, happiness, and take the wind

Like ashes scattered on a stormy day,
Since treason blows its poison in my soul.

ELFRIDA.

Thou art no traitor, though thyself shouldst say it,
For I did see a traitor once, my lord,
Who, by my father apprehended, stood
Some minutes in the circle of my eye.
I will not hear thee do thyself the wrong
To say thou art a traitor. Pray, my lord,
Wilt thou not find my horse?

ATHELWOLD.

                      He is not here,
The rebel rogue that threw you from his back.
We'll have him executed.

ELFRIDA.

                      Nay, my lord,
I think he'd find a way to get me back——

ATHELWOLD.

I beg you mount my horse. See how his eyes
Look so contemptuously on me now.
There is no management will keep him pent
Within the proper bounds of pride.
                              [*Exeunt.*

ACT II.

SCENE I.—ORDGAR'S CASTLE IN DEVONSHIRE.

Ordgar *and* Judith. *A Servant.*

Judith.

My lord, where is Elfrida?

Ordgar.

Caged.

Judith.

Caged, my lord? You wander.

Ordgar.

Not I, nor yet our daughter. When she roves,
It is to wed Lord Gafney. Set your head
As firmly as you will, you'll find it so.

Judith.

She will not wed him.

ORDGAR.

No? She will not wed him? Will she not?
This Athelwold hath asked me for her hand,
Wherein he pressed a losing claim. At that
I find them plotting, fuming, sighing, sick.
I send her to her chamber; there she stays
Until she wed Lord Gafney.

JUDITH.

'Tis not a month since thou wert in a rage
Because my lord of Gafney urged his suit
Upon the like account. Now in your grace,
Now off, now on. By our true faith, my lord,
If that be reason, what must folly be?

ORDGAR.

I say she shall not wed Lord Athelwold.
If that be folly, what must reason be?

JUDITH.

My lord, what blemish dost thou find in him
That stands in opposition to his suit?

ORDGAR.

Still punishing that string!

JUDITH.

What in his state condition, dignity,
Canst thou condemn, and honor still thyself?

ORDGAR.

I will not hear to it. That's my reason.

JUDITH.

Why, that's no reason, but the lack of it;
And I could give thee fifty reasons flat
To show that 'tis no reason.

ORDGAR.

Elfrida shall not wed Lord Athelwold;
So much is absolute. A hanger-on
And emissary of that English king—
God save him!—who has robbed me of my land
Shall never wed my daughter. Hear you that?

JUDITH.

Why, how ungently you do pick me up!
I would thou'rt not so testy. 'Tis no fault—
And you must know it—of Lord Athelwold
That Edgar wrongs you, robs you of your land.

ORDGAR.

Why, I did win it in a dozen fights,
And paid no court to rest nor drowsy night,
But fought them as I would another foe;
Quarrelled with insolent November winds,
And vexed the chilled and half-congealèd streams
With the rude opposition of my limbs,
Till I am better fit to hug the hearth
And fight old battles with my ready tongue
Than coax the venture still of fresh exploits.
But yet I bore no malice toward my foes,
Having all proper Christian grudges paid
In open battle. Now it gallops off,
A forfeit to the king! Out on such kings!
Tut! I'll have none of them, no rogue of them.

JUDITH.

My lord, he hath your figure, face, and form,
And as you were Lord Athelwold is now;
For in such correspondence are you set
That I do think these two, with all my heart,
Were made to give our lives continuance.

ORDGAR.
                      And there it is again.
I cannot sneeze but you do whisper me,

"So sneezed Lord Athelwold on such a day;"
If he doth whistle, stand you by and swear,
"So puckered I my mouth in frisky youth,
When wanton joy slid piping through my lips."
Little or much or nothing, let me be
Myself, and, though it be or beat the devil,
Kick the pattern in the sea. Have I eyes?
"So has Lord Athelwold." Have I a nose?
"Lord Athelwold has one." Must I take food?
"By heaven, Lord Athelwold doth likewise eat."
As if 'twere something from the expected course
That we should both have noses and need food!

Enter LORD GAFNEY.

Good-morrow, Gafney. Thou art not belied.
Holding thy foes so lightly in esteem,
'Tis said thou fearest no man. Fearest thou no woman?

GAFNEY.

I fear no woman, sir, doth meditate
A trial of my valor.

ORDGAR.

Well, sir, I have a daughter. (*To a servant.*) Fetch
her here.   [*Exit* Servant.

GAFNEY.

'Tis a good thing to have, my lord.

ORDGAR.

Well, I have a daughter——

GAFNEY.

A most delightful acquisition, sir,
Wherein I am deficient, having no wife.

ORDGAR.

And, sir, she hath no husband for her hand.

GAFNEY.

A pity for the husband that might be.

ORDGAR.

Lord Gafney?

GAFNEY.

I have not left, my lord.

ORDGAR.

Art thou afraid to jump, lest thou shouldst strike
On thy desire, or dost thou lack in wit?

Gafney.

Art thou afraid to offer me Elfrida,
Or dost thou lack in speech? Alas, my lord,
'Twould please me well if she might be my wife;
But, sir, I see the ground is occupied.

Enter Elfrida.

Elfrida.

I am your loving daughter, by command
Brought here from prison to inquire thy will.

Ordgar.

Elfrida, not a prison. Nay, that's wild;
Speak not so foolishly. Thy chamber 'tis,
Next to my own, whence thou wert wont to call,
From a wee child, for kisses in the night,
And never wert refused. It was my hand
Did trail the lazy creeping vines to cross
In curious tangle o'er thy window, lest
The dallying Sun-god kiss and wake thee up,
Ere he had swept the vapors for my child.
And now, because I send you to its rest,
It is a prison.

ELFRIDA.

Oh, sir, and I do wrong you cruelly.
Forgive me. 'Tis no prison, but a place
That with a hundred tongues approves your love.

ORDGAR.

Why, that is dutiful,—my love deserved.
Address this good and worthy gentleman.

ELFRIDA.
      Lord Gafney—

GAFNEY.

Sweet lady, save thy tears, thy quivering words,
To speak of one who does not love you.

ELFRIDA.

They are, my lord, for him who loves me most;
The piteous witnesses of royalty.

GAENEY.

And witness, therefore, of allegiance mine.

ELFRIDA.

Divided ligeance doth despise the law,
And that's my answer to your urgency.

ORDGAR.

Elfrida, nay. It is no answer meet.
What! well, but thou shalt. Not much is sure,
But here's a little scrap of certainty.
Go make you ready for the marriage. Go!

ELFRIDA.

    Make ready? When?

ORDGAR.

I care not when, nor what the time you choose,
But let it be a certainty.

ELFRIDA.

        Oh, sir, no.

ORDGAR.

No? Why, here's perversity. "Oh, sir, no"!
I'll "no" you, nobody!

GAFNEY.

    My lady——

ELFRIDA.

Oh, fear hath stol'n the blushes from my cheeks,
Else were I hid behind that crimson armor

From my purchaser. But, Gafney, you, a man!
Say, what's my price, Lord Gafney, what's my price,—
How many days thou'lt dig the fields for me?
Oh no, thou wilt not dig,—that takes a man,—
But thou'lt be chambermaid, the cook perchance.
How thou wilt stand with dish——

Ordgar.

Why, what a tempest have we here untied!
Come, come, be reasonable, idiot!

Gafney.

I swear you wrong me, lady, that you do.
No other fee than honorable love
In daily bounties rendered to yourself,
And so much honor as my hands can wring
From out the iron grip of ramping war,
Is offered for you or is worthy you.
Nor in the advantage of the earl's consent,
But as my warranty, do I stand clothed;
For I'd not buy or get a maiden's heart
At any other market than her own,
Believe me.

Elfrida.

Pray you, let me go. I'm ill.

[*Exit.*

ORDGAR.

She's gone.

GAFNEY.

It scarce needs telling, sir; she's gone. Farewell.
[*Exit.*

ORDGAR.

So much befall these sick, perturbèd fools
With more of reason in a mullet skull
And senseless chatter of the lousy apes.
If so, so good. If not, cords round their napes.

JUDITH.

I fear me thou art ill. Is it so, my love?

ORDGAR.

These importunities have made me so,
And I am irritated, racked, and grieved,
And cumbered up with idle arguments.
I tell thee, woman, I am old and dried,
But I can mind me when 'twas otherwise.

JUDITH.

Not old, my lord. Oh no! Speak not of age.
My love doth trudge along as fast as time,

And hath a constant variableness,
Changing each year as thou dost yearly change.
Ere love for thy dear self can well abate,
The jugglery of Time hath changed thy hair,
Added new wrinkles, dear, upon thy brow,
Till thou'rt another husband, and my love
Pays its devotion to the new-found god.
All these mutations are the gifts of time,
Which keep our fickle hearts forever fond.

ORDGAR.

Well, have thy way, so thou art sure of this.
I tell thee, Judith, he's a noble youth,
And thou shalt have thy way. I know a trick
Will set me even with the world again.
You wish it: be it so. Lord Athelwold
Shall wed Elfrida.

ELFRIDA (*without*).

     Yes, I would, my lord.
The lofty agitation which doth stir
The peremptory hearts of crownèd queens
Is next to that which moves the eternal Mind
When from the hidden places of His might
He wheels the noiseless enginery of worlds
To fill the barren heavens with huge spheres.

ATHELWOLD (*without*).

Too wild in imagery for sweet content.
Why covet these impossibilities,
Which those who gain them find so little worth?

ELFRIDA.

Oh no.

Enter ATHELWOLD *and* ELFRIDA.

ORDGAR.

Here come these errant rogues again.
Elfrida, dost thou love this gentleman?
What say you now, my gentle Athelwold?
Now, what a robbed and gutted store am I!
The king did take my land,—take you my loss;
Who being amicable with the king,
I turn my loss upon his nearest friend.
Thus lightly fall heaven's vengeance on us all.
But you do rob me of my daughter now;
Her mother robs me of my will. So I
But lose my loss in you, and gain a son,
And do not need my will. Nay, blush not so.
I saw that blush upon thy mother's cheek
Before we wed, and have not seen it since;
So I am even, gaining as I lose. [*Exeunt.*

SCENE II.—THE PALACE.

Enter KING EDGAR, ATHELWOLD, *and* OSRIC.

KING EDGAR.

And now, my good and noble Athelwold,
My passions, curious as chambermaids,
Do crowd within the portals of my ear
To hear what thou wouldst tell my better part
Of our Elfrida, rose of Devonshire.

ATHELWOLD.

My liege, if she were gracious Edgar's queen,
My eyes were subject as my spirit is.

KING EDGAR.
        Well?

ATHELWOLD.

And, being queen, thy love would make her fair.

KING EDGAR.

Nay, being fair, my love shall make her queen.

ATHELWOLD.

All women have some beauty. What of that?
For wives more fair than mothers less are loved,
And beauty, pleasing when the world was young,
Hath multiplied, repeated, grown to be
The cheapest salable commodity,
A gaud for rustics to display at fairs,
The only curtain which conceals the soul.

KING EDGAR.

My lord, thy tongue's a booby messenger
That jigs before thy mind till lazy wit
Can dress itself and open up the door.
You hint it like a participle, man.
Come out.

ATHELWOLD.

My lord, you set me to a bitter task
When I should one disparage whom Your Grace
Hath held in ignorant estimate as worth
Your royal favor.

KING EDGAR.

        Why, I like not this.

ATHELWOLD.

Then,—for I love Your Highness,—this fair maid,
Which so in courtesy my tongue declares,
I would not have her to be England's queen,
In such regard I hold Your Majesty,
Though I were thereby king of twenty realms
As rich in dignity as this I serve.

KING EDGAR.

Still tonguing it! What's her defect, my lord?
For such there are as call her beautiful.

ATHELWOLD.

No doubt. I grant you, when her face is still,
The fervent swain on whom her heart is set
Doth call her beautiful.

KING EDGAR.

     Pray, who is that?

ATHELWOLD.

I do not know him. A dishonest lout,
A lord of some degree. What is his name?
No matter: he's a fool. But when she speaks,
Her face doth never know the thing she says

And help to tell it; while her mournful teeth—
Those time-stained monuments of vanished sweets—
Do warn the hasty lover to beware.
And when she sits, in attitude uncouth,
One leg rides free and swings upon its mate.
Her harsh, unmaidenly, untunèd voice
Scratches like sand upon the inmost ear.
She hath no grace nor wantonness in limb,
Wit in her eye, nor dimple in her cheek;
Gloss on her hair, nor meaning in her laugh;
Play in her breast, nor cunning in her smile——

King Edgar.

Hold, hold, my lord, for I am satisfied.

Athelwold.

Pardon, my liege, but 'neath her frowzy hair
And in her bosom are the blemishes
Of a she-fiddler or a gipsy camp.

King Edgar.

No more, I beg you. 'Tis enough, enough;
Though slow in coming, long shall it remain,
And, ten times more, I would not wed her still.
No skill could paint her coarse enough for that;

So rest you from your weary journeying,
And I shall meet my council, quitting love
Until my stomach's stronger. [*Exit.*

ATHELWOLD.

Oh, how my tongue should blister for these lies,
My sweet Elfrida, who and heaven forgive!
For she is glorious when she doth speak.
Her face insists upon the thing she says.
Her voice is soothing, sweet, and musical.
She hath soft grace and wantonness of limb,
Gloss in her hair, and meaning in her laugh.
Beneath her crown of glory, and bound up
Within her gracious bosom, are the gems
That would enrich a hundred crownèd queens.
Her heart's the harbor of love's argosies,
Where those fair ships may lie, nor be betrayed
To restless winds that sweep the outer seas;
There, all unvexed, their golden freight unlade,
Till life shall seek its native skies again
And warmly motion love to come. Amen!
And that's my rosary, which, backward conned,
'Tis said doth call the devil. This, for once,
Hath sent him shivering home again to hell.

SCENE III.—THE PALACE.

Enter KING EDGAR *to a* MESSENGER.

KING EDGAR.

Be off, indifferent messenger, begone!
Two days have died and rot before your nose,
And you can sniff the stink in patience! Go!

MESSENGER.

My noble lord, 'tis true the days are dead,
But I have killed them with my busy deeds.
I have returned within the hour. I find
The message to Your Highness is most true:
Lord Athelwold is with Elfrida wed.

KING EDGAR.

You have my leave to go.
Huh! huh!
"I would not have her to be England's queen
For twenty"—was it twenty?—"realms like this"
I think he would not: he did speak the truth.
O honest Athelwold, to speak the truth!
And men do wed with such a graceless wench,

If they can get 'em, and persuade 'em to it.
Perhaps: I'll go and see—I'll go and see.
And if! *if!* IF!   A raging fool am I!
" I would not have her to be England's queen
For twenty realms like this" !   The very words,
Abating not a hiss nor syllable.
[*Exit.*

SCENE IV.—THE PALACE.

Philip, Sancie, *and another* Servant.

Philip.

If there be not something gone wrong, with His Majesty off unawares and the wolves all killed, whereby the Welsh have much gain, then I'm nobody.

Servant.

How now, Philip? More wonders to puzzle thy head and frighten the unwary?

Sancie.

There's more things that never happened than what has.

SERVANT.

Why, there lies his proficiency,—in things that never came to pass.

PHILIP.

What! (*To Sancie.*) Get thee gone, slut, to the cookery! What knowest thou of astrology? Get thee away, friz-pate, to thy pots and thy pans!

SANCIE.

Nay, but I'll get me not hence till the humor takes me. Now, mind thee that, thou bald-headed blunder and a scald-bald!

PHILIP.

No? Thou wilt not? Then thou shalt stay and cook dinner for those who rise at the judgment.

SANCIE.

And I'll not stay at thy bidding.

PHILIP.

Ay, and right here thou shalt continue. If thou be not ready when the old kings rise who have fasted some hundreds of years, look to thy soul, Saneie, look to thy soul! Oh, they'll grip thee and bite thee——

SANCIE.

Ooh! oo-o!

SERVANT.

Out, ye ape, and let shame rub thy heart to a blister! If thou hadst a hair more on top of thy head and bore thyself with a hair more of propriety, thou wouldst indeed be something.

PHILIP.

And now, if I had a hair more on top of my head and bore myself with a hair more of propriety, what would I be?

SERVANT.

Then thou wouldst be a monkey. [*Exit.*

SANCIE.

Ee-he-he-getts! that was a good one!

PHILIP.

Thou tatter-head! I have said better many's the time. Is it not so? Come now, Sancie, wouldst thou not like to be a sharp man as I am, to say pinching things and make men stare?

Sancie.

Lord, I have the ambition, but if I had the ideas!
Now thou didst only jest about the starved kings?

Philip.

Ay. I hope they are well fed where they are, and
will not stay to dinner. So fare thee well, Sancie, and
keep thy wrath till I turn liar and call thee young and
beautiful. [*Exit.*

Sancie (*singing*).

Men do roam the world around
 To find a wife whom they can trust·
While maidens wait till they are found
 And take whoever coaxes most.
[*Exit.*

Enter Osric *and* Edmund.

Edmund.

Is this departure of my lord the king
Not something hastily concluded on,—
A coltish humor spurred beyond its speed,
With belly full of undigested grain?

Osric.

'Twas long enough, but most unwisely pondered.
He hath of late been somewhat——

EDMUND.
                              Not——
OSRIC.
No, not as one might say,—
Yet in a sort of melancholy way,
He hath put on a mask of merriment
Which, dropping frequently, and then again
Put on as in confusion, showed a mind
That coaxed some vagrant purpose which himself
Held in disfavor.

EDMUND.
          That I noted not,
But in the manner of his going off.
Oh, well, he hath not been himself, indeed,
This little while   Methinks the king is ill.

OSRIC.
When he is ill, then is he most himself;
Who, being well, doth hospitably lodge
A spirit riotous and most perverse,
Which having bound his several faculties
And freed a chainèd host of boisterous fiends,
They hold a daily revel in his heart.
The king is well, which is his sorest ill;

And he hath gone this day to Devonshire,
Bent on the Lord knows what and I may guess.

Edmund.

It is not new that you do rate him so,
Waiting occasions when his feet slip up
To spread his faults upon the palace walls
And show them like a picture.

Osric.

       Hark you now,
For I do know a thing, and it is true:
Not long ago was Athelwold dispatched
To see old Ordgar's daughter, whom report
Did say was lovely as a summer's dawn,—
For Edgar, having given up his crown
To Dunstan on the nun's account, did think
To choose himself a good and lawful queen,—
But Athelwold did cover her with smut
And hide her beauty in his heart, his tongue
Meanwhile diverting Edgar's mind
With most unwholesome conjuring and lies:
This I did hear myself, and know it true.
Then pops he off and marries her himself,
Which, coming to the knowledge of the king,

Engendered purposes presaging ill
To Athelwold, whom he did truly love.

EDMUND.
              I do not blame the king.

OSRIC.
Nor I Lord Athelwold. 'Tis said the girl
Might well seduce cold Dunstan from his vows;
And Athelwold is not a chunk of ice,
But flesh and nerves and possibilities
That loudly claim a hearing in the world.

EDMUND.
              I do not know.

OSRIC.
I know. I say Lord Athelwold did well.
The king himself could not have bettered it,
And he is skilful in the like pursuits.   [*Exit.*

EDMUND.
This Osric gossips with a woman's tongue,
And man's advantage to acquaint himself,
As confident in his conjecturings
As one who once hath guessed a hidden truth
And thinks himself inspired with prophecy.
                            [*Exit.*

ACT III.

SCENE I.—ATHELWOLD'S CASTLE.

Enter ATHELWOLD, EGBERT, *and* ROGER.

EGBERT.

My lord, His Gracious Majesty, the king,
Hath, by his special favor, singled you
So far that in your castle he will bide.

ATHELWOLD.

I am much honored by His Majesty.
When comes he?

EGBERT.

    Ere the setting of the sun,
If no mishap.

ATHELWOLD.

So soon? Yes, yes, and I am honored much.

EGBERT.

And I am weary, and I fain would rest.

ATHELWOLD.

Yes, Roger, 'tis a royal messenger
Who brings us welcome tidings of the king,
The odor of a joy not far removed,
And thereby hath the honor of a king.

EGBERT.

Thanks, Lord Athelwold.   [*Exit.*

ATHELWOLD.

Too well—too well for happiness—I know
The frame and constitution of the man.
If some delay by storm or flood were had,
So that but one poor day might serve mv will,
This business might be fashioned to my lie.
But see those rascal skies, that now deny
Their early-morning promises of rain.
I know a way, an excellent device;
She will not do it; I must ask too much.
Yet less is ruin.   How will Dunstan laugh
To see how poorly my allegiance yields!
Oh, cursed charm of beauty! only that

Which is the least and poorest in degree
Of all the virtues gives a husband fear.

Enter ELFRIDA.

ELFRIDA.
Why looks my lord so troubled?

ATHELWOLD.
To-day, my love, the king doth visit us.

ELFRIDA.
The king! Fair fall the way before His Grace!
Yet am I with a hundred doubts perplexed
How we, who are but subject, may put on
A guise that shall delight His Majesty,
For he will look at me and haply think
That I am fair. What think you, Athelwold,—
That he may bend his royal thoughts so far
As thinking I am beautiful?

ATHELWOLD.
Oh, love that thou shouldst wish him think you so!

ELFRIDA.
May be a sigh he is not Athelwold.

ATHELWOLD.

Now, as thou lovest me, uproot that wish
Ere it doth put another blossom forth.

ELFRIDA.

What! shall the oak be jealous of the sun
Because the lily in his favor stands?
Or shall the brown earth, like a fool, slight off
His warm smiles in the harvest? Oh, my lord!

ATHELWOLD.

          Dost thou not love me?

ELFRIDA.

More than life I do; and so this morn,
And yesternight, and many times each day,
My lips have told you; and my love doth run
Before your questions, saying, "I am here."

ATHELWOLD.

It is no task for love to yield its will.

ELFRIDA.

How soberly you bear yourself to-day!
Love hath no will, and never yields to will.

ATHELWOLD.

But love would do as much as love could ask?

ELFRIDA.

It is not kind that you should question so
The quality of my obedience,
Or test my love by half-concealèd doubts
In sombre interrogatories veiled.
I have not tried to render what is due,
Nor estimated what your love is worth,
But, in exchange, have given all I had,
And do it willingly, and will do more
If you will show me how.

ATHELWOLD.

It breaks my heart that I must ask so much
That seems of demonstration but the proof;
Yet, I beseech you, in your coarsest garb
And slovenly attire array yourself,
And from your meanest servant borrow airs;
Put carmine in your eyes to make them red,
And let a smutch of brown defile your ears.
Make harsh and rough as sand your heavenly
    voice——

ELFRIDA.

My lord, my love, you know not what you ask,
But hold me as a woman of the town.
I am your wife, and have no charms to sell,
For they are yours, not mine, and are secure
Though you should throw them back again to me.

ATHELWOLD.

I swear I do believe you.   Nay, 'twere true
And evident without the saying.
Doubting, my heart had never found a voice
Until it came to say " Farewell."   Oh, sweet
And blessed lady, born with that dear gift
Of alchemy which turns a leaden grief
To purest gold of happiness and trust,
This last and only fear——

ELFRIDA.

I will not hear you,—will not barter words
When you conceive that I am marketed.
Oh, I could tear my ears from off my head,
And would have done it had I guessed your thought,
Rather than hear you question me.

ATHELWOLD.

I swear again you wrong me and yourself
By these misapprehensions. Cease your tears;
Believe that I have reasons which the times
Forbid my telling even to my soul,
Yet draw no tint nor sparkle from your love.
Can you believe it?

ELFRIDA.

       'Tis beyond belief,
But love must sometimes seek those giddy deeps.
You hug an evident delusion, love,
Whose name and features sanity would shun.
Therefore am I persuaded, Athelwold,
That this most witless humor of my lord
Will, like all folly, go so far in quest
Of some approving reason presently
That it shall lose itself and not return.
And, meanwhile, with the nicest-ordered care
I will array myself in such a guise
As may become the wife of Athelwold.

ATHELWOLD.

I do beseech you call it folly, then,
Which is, and since the world was made hath been,

The darling price which wisdom pays for love.
Do what I ask, and call it what you will.
Did ever love refuse so small a thing
As that it should secure itself from harm
And hide behind a folly?

ELFRIDA.

Pray give some reason,—one; and, though it be
Too weak, impalpable, to touch the soul,
If it but hover near my consciousness
I may consent; but otherwise I know
'Tis ruinous jealousy, the sifting dust
Of dead and musty love filling your eyes.
And with so mean a passion argument
Doth but undo itself.

ATHELWOLD.

Oh, Elfrida!

ELFRIDA.

You were about to speak?

ATHELWOLD.

The truth is sweet for ever, but a lie
Is good for one day only. Hear my tale.
Do you remember when I saw you first?

ELFRIDA.

It has not been so long I could forget.

ATHELWOLD.

To serve the king I came to Devonshire,—
That lustful king who from her holy vows
At Wilton wrung the pure, devoted nun
And made her tears his laughter, mocked her vows,
And held her to his pleasure.

ELFRIDA.

And would she not be queen? Can there be one
Who would so high a dignity refuse?

ATHELWOLD.

She was the Holy Church's willing bride;
Yet had she been as free as once thou wert,
She would have scorned the doubtful honor down
Unless her heart had with her head been crowned.
It was to serve this king I sought you out,
For he had heard how beautiful thou art,
And me dispatched to see if this were true.

ELFRIDA.

                Is that true?

Athelwold.

That thou art beautiful?

Elfrida.

That he did send you on that mission?

Athelwold.

'Tis true, my love, and true it is I came,
And from that moment could not speak the truth.
I did report you all that you are not,
Made light of graces that the Graces shame,
And with repugnance toward you filled his soul,—
If he possess a soul; but this I doubt.

Elfrida.

And but for this I might have been the queen?

Athelwold.

But for this fault you had not been my wife.

Elfrida.

False, treacherous scum! that did deceive the king
And steal such honor from your wife's own head!
Time rests his chin upon his scythe and winks
To see how short a liar makes his way.

ATHELWOLD.

Oh, say my love was stronger than the truth,
That thou wert cheated into happiness
And I have lied my way to heaven.

ELFRIDA.

That lie hath war and discord made in heaven,
And set my faculties at variance.

ATHELWOLD.

For me repeat the lie and make it truth,
And think how often we did envy sleep,—
Which is the thief of happy consciousness —
Murmured at brief enforcèd absences,
Quarrelled with time, that dallied by the way,
Then say, "He is more human than I knew."
But if you have regrets, they are not vain.
Here is my dagger; all my blood's a lie.
Your gross unkindness splits my very heart,
And this were balm. I do not fear its use.
Turn from me with your eyes. I'll try its point.

ELFRIDA.

And have I come so low as wounding you?
I thank you for that blessed perjury.

Henceforth for you I shall believe all lies,
And love them, swearing they are more than truth.
Forgive me, though it strain your heart to do it.
I am more hateful than you told the king,
And shall strip off the mask you call so fair
And let my scullion soul to him appear.
[Exit.

Enter ROGER.

ATHELWOLD.

Is Egbert well bestowed?

ROGER.

Comfortably, sir.

ATHELWOLD.

That is a harp, good Roger?

ROGER.

It is, sir.

ATHELWOLD.

A single string doth yield no harmony,
But, like a life unmated, strikes the soul
Of all the listening world and gives no joy.

ROGER.

There is no discord in a single string.

ATHELWOLD.

No discord, and no harmony; one tone,—
One poor heart-wearying and depressing note.

ROGER.

        Yes.

ATHELWOLD.

Good Roger, I am somewhat sad to-day;
The king is coming, yet I am not gay.
I pray you let us have a merry song,
Which doth dissolve the grasp of hard Despair
And make him helpless.

ROGER.

      So we shall, my lord.

SONG.

  The shivering earth was out at play
    With Zephyr's brawling sister,
  Till late one day, in spangles gay,
    Jack Frost came down and kissed her.

How they danced!
Through the meadows how their light feet glanced,
   The earth with jewels strewing.
Oh, the virtuous moon shuts both her eyes
   When lovers go a-wooing.

No more she chased the frightened leaves
   To many a nook and hollow,
Nor harshly railed about the eaves
   To scare the trembling swallow.
      For they danced, etc.

The gentle oak, that loved the shrew
   Sighed for her rude embraces;
But what can jilted lovers do
   When rivals steal their places?
      Still they danced, etc.

ATHELWOLD.

Well?

ROGER.

That's all.

ATHELWOLD.

         It is enough.

ROGER.

It hath a meaning to it, though, my lord,
However rough and tuneless it may be;

For never have two lovers blessed the world
But that a third hath suffered for their love;
And so my song, and so my moral, ends.

ATHELWOLD.

Good-day, and thanks, good Roger, for your song.

ROGER.

Oh, that's all right.   [*Exit* ATHELWOLD.

Now, here is the prodigious merit of His Lordship, that he sees no wantonness, though the sun shine upon it. But blindness to the excellence of virtue,—oh, that's damnable! I'll write a book. That must not evaporate, and I'll find an application for it. Now there's Roxie. I have a good eye for a good thing; yet these two days she hath been all merriment but when I spoke, and then,—oh, how disdain did pinch her pretty mouth!

Enter ROXIE.

ROXIE.

Good-day, Roger; for I see if I be not the better, and speak, thou wouldst never look at me. Explain thyself, Sir Rogue, for a peevish lover.

ROGER.

Peevish, and not look at you? No.

ROXIE.

I say 'tis true, and worthy of a clown
That you deny it. You do know 'tis true.

ROGER.

Indeed, I know I did not speak with you,
For proud Disdain did cover both your ears,
And kiss your lips to keep your answer back,
When I began to speak.

ROXIE.

      A jealous babe!

ROGER.

A jealous babe, and jealous of disdain!

ROXIE.
      Go away!

ROGER.
           Away?

ROXIE.

Go away!

ROGER.

What trickery hath foolish Cupid played,
To tip his arrow with such bitterness?
What's in the wind? 'Tis not thy pretty self—
And yet I know not who—to crimp thy brow,
And let the pouting imps disfigure you.
Now, what's the matter?

ROXIE.

    Oh, I know not what,
Unless it be to have you ask me what,
So I may say 'tis nothing. If I frown
Or seem obdurate, or if I do weep,
Then is it so because I know not why,
And weep the more, more wanting an excuse.
Then with hard-pressed inquiries flatter me,
And apprehensive eyes, and coaxing words,
And consolation for imagined woes.

ROGER.

Why, on my life, that suits me mightily,
For never yet did woman coaxing love

So well as I to wheedle and to tease.
Your frown's a white cloud in a summer sky,
Your wrath but pleasant singing, and your smile
An answer to all reasonable prayers.

ROXIE.

For that I'll tell you something. Hear me now;
But if you say, "I knew it," and you will,—
Oh, that's a man, it is, for all the land,
To pocket up his thumbs, and say, "Oh, that?
I knew that long ago," when he didn't,—
But, if you do, be your own chronicle.

ROGER.

What is it you will tell me?

ROXIE.

I will not tell you; you will say you knew it.

ROGER.

     My word I will not.

ROXIE.

To-day the king is coming. Stand you there
As if he came like sunrise? Cackle, goose,

And say you knew it! I know better, though.
Now, Roger, did you?

ROGER.

My word, my word! I've pledged it not to say.

ROXIE.

Bear your own candle, then. I'll wed a woman,
And if she knows, as very like she will,
She'll be no goose, to mar the telling so.

[Exit.

ROGER.

Marry a woman, hey? I'll do the same.
She'll change her mind before she does her name.

SCENE II.—ATHELWOLD'S CASTLE.

ELFRIDA *and* ROXIE.

ROXIE.

Sweet lady-love, be not so silly-slouched,
But put these jewels in your precious ears.
La! miserere! what is that, my pet,
That in this white and pinky vestibule

Hath found a lodgment? Oh, you shame your lord.
There, now! But wait. This joy hath kinked your
    head.
Now 'tis a porch where king's words may wait.

ELFRIDA.

To make sweet music to a silly queen
Who hath another lover. What was that?
Oh, I'm nobody. Do you love my lord?

ROXIE.

Why, this is madness.

ELFRIDA.

        Do you love my lord?

ROXIE.

As honors me and you, I love him well.

ELFRIDA.

Then take him. But beware if you do sleep,
For I will pin a dagger in your heart.

ROXIE.

Oh, sweetest, dearest ruin of my soul,
Where did you get this madness?

ELFRIDA.

Where the pale spheres hang trembling in the heavens,
Gasping to feel the immeasurable deeps
That struggle mightily to swallow them.
But 'tis no madness, for I know my mind
And speak in allegories; know a lie,
And can decipher truth in riddles hid.
You know it is no madness; 'tis the truth.
The daisies grow in spite of serpents' teeth,
And never see 'em. Are my jewels gone?
I care not; let him see me as I am.

ROXIE.

Nay, bathe your face, and do not be a child,
Refractory and stubborn; be a queen,
And give this laggard loving king to note
What stuff for consorts loyal knights do wear.

ELFRIDA.

You drive me mad! My love is steady true:
I would not waver for a million kings.
It is a fool who does not go himself.
But, Roxie, keep you from Lord Athelwold——

ROXIE.

Dear heart, chase these vagaries from your brain,

And coax them not again. It is a jest,
A cruel jest, which heartless fancy plays;
He seeks the weak, the sick, the innocent,
And scares them with his mimicry of truth.

ELFRIDA.

Nay, Roxie, I believe thou art a saint.
You think me jealous; I am only ill.
And, if I choose it, may I not be ill?
But I am better; leave me to myself.
Nay, do not look so frightfully on me.
I am not dangerous; I know my mind,
And here would rest an hour by myself.
[*Exit* ROXIE.
What's love? A baby. What is life? To be
Mighty and strong, and terrible as death.
(*Sees herself in the mirror.*)
Elfrida, thou art beautiful. Farewell!
Thou art not she the sun this morning kissed.
I know not who thou art, but feel a spirit
That hath Elfrida conquered in my breast.
[*Exit.*

SCENE III.—ATHELWOLD'S CASTLE.

Enter KING EDGAR *and* ELFRIDA.

KING EDGAR.

Shall we not have some music presently,
Which, like a blessed solvent, doth set free
The thick and heavy current of the brain?
For love, which reconciles the warring powers,
And sets the chainèd tongue of fancy free,
Hath bound my faculties and made me mute
In those soft, winsome phrases coveted.
It is the grief of kings that they are bounded
By such impediments as check their slaves,
Who, having needs exceeding common men,
And less of time to gain them, throw themselves
In ignorance upon a prop too frail.

ELFRIDA.

You do a little wander in your speech.

KING EDGAR.

It is because thou art so beautiful.

ELFRIDA.

Oh, thanks, my lord! And do you think me so?

KING EDGAR.

My eyes hold constant converse with my soul,
And wisdom thrives upon that amity.
But wisdom, which hath schooled me in desire,
Grows clownish, fickle, and unstably set
When I demand how much I dare to hope.

ELFRIDA.

'Tis foolishness in wisdom's garb, my lord,
For that would teach thee not to wish, but hope,
Nor love thy wish till love begets a fear
To risk it in an honorable test.

KING EDGAR (*aside*).

The wisdom summoned to persuade me on
Should teach her virtue. None so justly whelmed
As she who sees the coming of the flood
And opens the defences. (*To Elfrida.*) Know you
    the queen?

ELFRIDA.

Heaven rest her well, for she is not, my lord.

KING EDGAR.

She is in heaven, my lady,—she's in heaven;
But thou art here to grace and bless the world.

> Sweet be the flowers of Paradise:
> For these our spirits wait;
> But dearer to our earth-born eyes
> The rose outside the gate.

Be thou that lovely rose, which shall adorn
The palace of the king.

ELFRIDA.

A jest, my lord.

KING EDGAR.

Wilt thou not be my love?

ELFRIDA.

I am a wife.
You know you ask impossibilities.

KING EDGAR.

I am a king, not given to soft speech,
Nor versed in ways of wily argument.
A child might rest uneasy in these arms,

But I can hush with iron lullabies
The cooing or the crowing of my foes.

ELFRIDA.

What does this mean?

KING EDGAR.

It means no less, nor well could purpose more,
Than that I love you.

ELFRIDA.

                Have thy thoughts to-day
Encompassed Athelwold? Think you such thoughts
Could rest their damning weight upon my soul
And not destroy it?

KING EDGAR.

                'Twas no ill I spoke.
(*Aside.*)
Oh, what a rash and hasty fool am I!
This I must mend.
But Dunstan, mark you, I shall close his mouth,
For I do love you, and the devil himself
Had better have a care. Dunstan I know,
But we shall fear not him.

ELFRIDA.

        You love me so?
My lord, I do not love you,—could not do it.
I am a wife; but if these bonds were strong,
And traps lie hid within a silken law,
That love might never look where wrong is done,
And make it worse for me than crowns could mend,
Or homage from the princes of the world,
So dear desire might well forget itself,
And none should ever come to it,—no! Well,
I pray you let me go; I'm ill.

KING EDGAR.

         No, stay.
If not the queen, 'tis better than a queen
To be a chosen rival, stamping out
The haughty glance of royal princesses,
And yet a subject greater than a queen.

ELFRIDA.

Is that your love? Now dare I trust myself.

KING EDGAR.

I cannot float upon such subtle waves.

Elfrida.

Then sink, thou puppy of a six days' growth!
For I did dream a moment; now I wake.
I cannot trust to know the words I said;
But, if I did not curse you, do I now.
I am a woman, Edgar; you're a fool!   [*Exit.*

King Edgar.

The wind hath quickly changed from west to north.
So let it blow; 'twill change again as quick
When Athelwold tunes up his golden harp.
'Twill change again.   Yes.
(Elfrida *passes into an adjoining room and meets* Athelwold.)

Athelwold.

Whence came you? for I think the king will storm
And hold me answerable.   Haste you now,
And fit you for his eyes.   Impatiently
He waits your presence with suspicious mind,
And holds your last night's illness as a cheat
Of my concoction.

King Edgar.

"I would not have her to be England's queen
For twenty realms like this."   The very words.

ELFRIDA.

Do not stop me here.

ATHELWOLD.

Nay, scowl not so.   Forgive me, dearest love.

ELFRIDA.

Out on such love!   Sour is born of sweet.
Pluck out this splinter from my hand.

ATHELWOLD.

Where is it?

ELFRIDA.

Nowhere.

ATHELWOLD.

Then your hand is well.

ELFRIDA.

Because there's no offender.   I am well
Because I have no love.   So get you gone.

ATHELWOLD.

You lead yourself, and thereby lose yourself.

ELFRIDA.

No one is lost who follows his nose.

ATHELWOLD.

Elfrida, these are unbecoming jests.
You are a lady, wife of Athelwold,
And have no need to play on idle words.

ELFRIDA.

Oh, I am merry. Let me be a clown.
And do not shut the door that shows my mind,
For that same door doth open up my heart.
I must be clown or devil. Let me play.

ATHELWOLD.

I do not know you.

ELFRIDA.

        I know you, my lord,—
A merry teasing liar and a fool,
Who, for his lady's sake, must daily be
Like sinful women, who do never mend,
But every day repent, pattern'd on me.

King Edgar.

"I would not have her queen for twenty realms."
He would not. Oh, he is an honest man

Athelwold.

Elfrida, you are not yourself to-day.
Put off your beauty as you do yourself;
The king may come this way and see you so.

Elfrida.

Ay, if he follows me.

Athelwold.

    Follows you?

Elfrida.

Go not in there. I left the king just now.

Athelwold.

      Elfrida!

Elfrida.

Speak louder, Athelwold; she's far away,
And I will go and find her for you.
       [*Exit.*

King Edgar.

He calls Elfrida, so her untuned voice,
Harsh and unmaidenly, may give reply.
I'll send you, Athelwold, into a realm
Worth many twenties such as this you serve.

Athelwold.

Betrayed! Oh, damned and execrable fate,
To buy a grave before my time because a rose
Doth bloom above it. Shamed and scouted at,
Stung, for a penny's worth of love, to death.
But I must see the king; he's waiting now.
Have I a dagger? Yes. I'll hold myself
All ready to defend my conscience now.
Where'er I go I'll take the king along.
   (*Enters to the king.*)

King Edgar.

Good-morrow, Athelwold, you merry rogue,
That "would not have her to be England's queen
For twenty realms as rich as this you serve."
Well done, my lord, well done! and you may laugh;
But had I guessed how well you played the rogue,
I could have easily outwitted you.
But let it go. It was a kingly trick,

And, like a king, I do forgive the jest,
And give you joy.   Here is my hand in peace.

ATHELWOLD.

Do you forgive me?

KING EDGAR.

Ay, for the glass which magnifies the offence
Is that which doth enlarge her beauty,—love.
So neither is as great as you conceive.
Thus I have claims on your forgiveness, too.
Can you forgive me?

ATHELWOLD.

With all my heart, and both are satisfied.

KING EDGAR.

Now having thus undone the tangled times,
And robbed your heart of needless jealousy,—
For I'll be bound you thought I'd love her too,—
We turn our minds to pleasure and the woods.
A profitable remnant still of time
Lies in the rear of our necessity,
Which we improve the meanwhile with our spears.
The savage boar invites our ardor now,
And we will waste to-morrow in his chase.

ATHELWOLD.

Your wish is mine.

KING EDGAR.
             Farewell, good Athelwold;
To-morrow we will hunt the savage boar.
                    [*Exit* ATHELWOLD.
Thou art too honest, gentle Athelwold,
To wed with such a sloven. Go to heaven,
And find a woman worthy of thy praise.
I'll send you there to-morrow, Athelwold,
Or, happily, the other way, curse you!

ACT IV.

SCENE I.—A FOREST IN DEVONSHIRE.

Enter KING EDGAR, ATHELWOLD, *and* DURK.

ATHELWOLD.

These tracks are newly stamped; he is not far.
See how this pale arbutus, faint with pain,
Lies crushed and rended, wishing it might die.

KING EDGAR.

Come on, come on! we hunt the ravenous boar.
What matter that the silly blossom aches,
Unless we kill the offender? What say you?

ATHELWOLD.

Even now he's ripping up the tender roots
Of birches, without license making this
His pasture. Or perchance this lady brook
Weeps farther on, that she must wash his hulk,
While he lies grunting, happy on her breast.

King Edgar (*aside*).

He gives me words, excuses.

Athelwold.

                    Ho! what's this?

Durk.

Ho-ho, my lord! Oh, murder! He-he-he!

Athelwold.

You untaught lout! what makes you merry now?

Durk.

Oh, sir, my lord, I cannot choose but laugh.
It's ripped. It looks so funny, lying there.

King Edgar.

Why brought you here this laughing fool along?
I am not pleased that this rude servitor
Should haunt us. Kick on his giggling shins,
And send him cackling off. Stop him, I say!

Athelwold.

Forgive him, sire, he doth not know a sin,
But in my heavier moments pleaseth me.
He is no fool, though he doth always laugh.

Come, Durk, why laugh you now? It is a bush
That hath been reft by violence.

DURK.

Oh, sir, fun tickles me, whereat my sides
And stomach roughly heave to oust the jade,
And my poor foolish mouth, which loves the sport,
Cries "Ha-ha!" to the merry combatants.
Oh, sir, my lord, for God's sake take 'em off,
And let 'em fight it out some otherwhere!
Oh, sir, I ache!

ATHELWOLD.

    Now up and go, good Durk;
And so I charge you, come not near to-day.
         [*Exit* DURK.

KING EDGAR.

Here go his feet. that lead from yonder copse.

ATHELWOLD.

Why, no, my lord, they lead across the brook.

KING EDGAR.

Say you I lie? Stand back, and lift your point.

Athelwold.

Tut! since you say it, he doth backward run.

King Edgar.

Nay, forward. Know I not the hateful track
Of that wild boar which devastates my park?
Look you! I say he came but now this way.

Athelwold.

Those are my feet. Alas! I see your mind.
Then, since I am a boar, to be pursued,
Still, like a boar, I'll turn and rend my foe,
Though he should be the king.

King Edgar.

Curses and death upon you, lying hound!
They know in hell I'm coming, but not now.
For many a day I shall enjoy thy love,
Whilst thou art squirming.

Athelwold.

                    Not too sure, my lord,
For I have more to live for than yourself,
And by so much the better can defend,—
As much of hate as thou, and more of skill.

KING EDGAR.

That's the way I hunt the boar.

ATHELWOLD.
And so he turns.
(*They fight.* ATHELWOLD *falls.*)

KING EDGAR.

I know you, Athelwold.   Beg not of me.

ATHELWOLD.

You never heard me beg.   Strike, rascal king,
That is his own vile executioner!
Now, since my lady proveth false to me,
For me she shall be doubly false to thee.

KING EDGAR.

He's dead.   So let the wild beasts bury him
In their sepulchral stomachs.   What care I?
[*Exit.*
(*Re-enter* DURK.)

DURK.

Ha-ha-ha-ha! upon my soul he's dead,
And these are spear-wounds that have injured him.
Alas that I should laugh to see him so!

But he hath curled his lip in such a sort,
As one who takes a bite of bitter-root,
Thinking it pleasant myrrh.
Oh, let me close this eye before I laugh,
To see it peeping so suspiciously.
Wow! didst thou stir? Oh, now I dare to laugh!
Oh, my dear master, and thou art not dead!
Now let me laugh upon thy dearest neck,
To see thou art alive.

ATHELWOLD.

Nay, let me lie;
You hurt me.

DURK.

Please forgive me.

ATHELWOLD.

Run for a litter; fetch your brothers here,
And they shall bear me to your cottage near.

SCENE II.—DURK'S HOME.

Enter DURK *and his* MOTHER. DURK *laughing*.

MOTHER.

Hush, you fool, and quit your laughing.
Why, what a working keg of wine are you
To sputter!

DURK.

Oh, stop me, calk me with a doleful psalm,
But one that is not said at funerals.
For I have heard the gloomy weepers howl,
And seen their tears, for one who is not dead.
I've seen a live man's funeral. Oh, he-e!

ATHELWOLD (*within*).

Durk!

MOTHER.

Lord Athelwold is calling. Come you in.
But, Durk, I tell you not to laugh. Now hear,
For he is like to die with those deep wounds.
Alas! I have my fears how they were got
Now keep in check, and tell him what he asks.

Enter to ATHELWOLD.

ATHELWOLD.

Whence came you?

DURK.

From your funeral.

ATHELWOLD.

Alas!
I would it had been so. When I am dead
Inter me decently; but let the bones
Of him who did usurp my very grave
Be honored, and enjoy my musty house.
Now tell me how my lady bore herself.

DURK.

It would have done you good to see her weep.

MOTHER.

Durk!

ATHELWOLD.

She had some tears for me? And was she sad?

DURK.

'Twas misery.

Mother.

My lord, I pray you, do not let her mourn.
Why, I do almost doubt my widowhood.
Though I myself his weary hands did fold,
And saw him buried, yet if it could be
That he as you——

Athelwold.

Hush, hush, good woman, your good man is dead.
Weep, if you will, but not for phantom joys.
Keep you and all your house my hidden life;
There is a purpose in it. Durk, my boy,
How is it I am buried?

Durk.

    Oh, my lord,
We brought you here as soon as you were hurt.
You bade us tell no one, nor did we do it;
But from the castle messengers were sent
To find your body. Falling on some bones
That looked as they were newly stripped of flesh,
They took them to your castle, buried them——

Athelwold.

Whose bones were they?

Durk.

I do not know, my lord; some traveller's.
We saw him but a day before your hurt.

Athelwold.

Now, Durk, if I do get my strength again,
Or if I do not, keep this in your heart:
Go not so often to the castle now,
But, on your going, keep yourself awake.

Durk.

I will.

Athelwold.

Now leave me. [*Exeunt.*
Rest, hapless thief, if thou didst envy me
The marble splendor of my resting-place.
Oh, when these limbs are at their wonted strength,
I'll make it good upon his murderous head
Who chose the spears, and gave me one whose point
Was softest lead, of tempered iron his.
Did she connive my death? It cannot be.
And would she wed with Edgar? Ay, she would
When one short year of lamentation's done;
But ere that time no Edgar shall there be.
I must compose myself to sleep.

SCENE III.—ATHELWOLD'S CASTLE.

Enter KING EDGAR *and* ELFRIDA.

KING EDGAR.

Let not these saucy, mud-nest birds of grief
Within so fair a temple rear their brood.
No angel is more provident than death,
Who neither way doth empty-handed fly;
For if he carries joy from earth to heaven,
He bears an equal weight from heaven to earth.

ELFRIDA.

Nay, do not comfort me, but let me weep;
And that the tears more freely still may run,
Relate again the manner of his death.

KING EDGAR.

'Tis said that grief can drown itself in tears,
And my own eyes shall help to swell the stream,
And bear her dead grief to the eternal seas.
When we had reached the stream I told you of,
He saw a little flower the boar had crushed,
And stopped to pity it.

ELFRIDA.

Oh, did he so?

KING EDGAR.

He did, my lady, and I wept myself
To think I e'er had envied such a soul,
And there embraced him, saying, "Athelwold,
Thou art more worthy of the sweetest rose
That on a mortal stalk did ever grow
Than I."

ELFRIDA.

Oh, thanks, my noble, noble king,
That did his last dear moment fill with joy.

KING EDGAR.

With rash and hardy indignation filled,
We did the brute pursue, I smiling oft
To see how tenderly he bore himself
Toward that poor laughing Durk who followed us.
At length, his gentle patience giving way,
He somewhat harshly bade the boy depart.
Nay, blame him not, though I did chide him then.
Scarce had the laughing slave departed, when,
With gleaming tusks and horrid frightful eyes,
Two boars came snorting from a neighboring copse.

ELFRIDA.

Oh, mercy!

KING EDGAR.

These charging at his legs tripped up his feet,
And down he fell breast foremost on his spear.

ELFRIDA.

Oh, heaven!

KING EDGAR.

Meanwhile my spear did drive the beasts away,
That else had torn him with their dreadful teeth.
Then decently composing all his limbs,
And hearing how the swine were scampering
Across and through the forest far away,
I left him there, and straightway came for help.
The rest you know,—how, ere the day was done,
And messengers could bring his body hence,
The thieving birds and beasts had stol'n his shape,
Leaving his weary bones alone to bring.

ELFRIDA.

Alas!

King Edgar.

And why alas, when I do love you so?

Elfrida.

Your love for me is not my love for him.

King Edgar.

Why, I did love him too, and never more
Than on that day his blessed spirit rose.
No friend have I, no faithful counsellor.
How often I recall that pretty trick
By which he thought he had offended me!
In faith he did, but I forgave it him,
As I bethought me of your happiness.
Alas! I am no man like Athelwold,
But I am king of England, and a man.
Canst thou not love me somewhat for his sake?

Elfrida.

I love the king, as duty doth demand.

King Edgar.

Forget the king; 'tis Edgar claims your love.

Elfrida.

I love the king, not Edgar.

King Edgar.

Let your love hang where it will.
Then wed the king, and Edgar's satisfied.

Elfrida.

Nay, leave me with my grief a single year.
'Tis not a week since Athelwold was here,
And I am in no mood to think of love,
For grief is sweeter than your love could be.

King Edgar.

Then let us grieve together; I am sad,
For I have lost a brother, you your love.

Elfrida.

I cannot hear you now; a month, my lord.

King Edgar.

No, not a month, nor yet a weary week.
Bury your grief within my heart of grief,
And let to-morrow be our wedding-day.

Elfrida.

To-morrow?

KING EDGAR.

To-morrow, lady, I must seek the court.
Wilt thou not hold thyself to go with me?

ELFRIDA.

To-morrow, then, since you do will it so,
And till to-morrow let me take my leave.
         [*Exit.*

KING EDGAR.

'Tis true, a woman's heart is like the ground,
That daily blooms with roses neat and trim;
Yet when one lord is gone, another found,
It yields as bounteously and free for him.
Yes; now I must remember how he died.
The boars came out and tripped him; then he fell
And struck his bosom on his spear. That's it.
This story gives me infinite relief:
I was afraid I killed him. That's the way:
The boars came out and tripped him off his feet,
And when he fell his bosom struck the spear.

SCENE IV.—THE PALACE.

Enter Dunstan *and* Elfrida *from opposite sides.*

Dunstan.

Good-morrow, madam. [*Exit.*

Enter King Edgar.

Elfrida.

A month, my lord, since I have been your wife,
And know not yet if I am queen or not.
In all the land are none so low as I.
See how your haughty bishop rears himself
Above the very front of dignity,
And says, "Good-morrow, madam," passing by,
Stuffed with such meditations of his might
That majesty itself seems mean and small.
And so it is. Your nobles plot and fume,
To see how tamely royalty doth bend
Before this impudent and knavish priest.

King Edgar.

The archbishop of Canterbury.

ELFRIDA.

The archbotcher of royalty. My lord,
Thou art the grandson of brave Athelstan,
He Alfred's son. When still a little child
I read the triumphs of these mighty men,
The lords of earls who life-long glory won
In greedy battle, hungry for the blood
Of pagan foemen who for spoils had come.
The morning saw five warlike youthful kings:
The evening saw them, by your father's sword,
In dreamless slumber lying. These were kings!
No tricksy priest dared ride upon the neck
Of warriors who could make the field resound,
And all the stiff intentions of the foe
Dissolve in their own blood.

KING EDGAR.
      Semiramis!
Well donè, my lady! Spoken like a queen!
Now let the Danes come on, we'll ride 'em down!
What would you have me be?—and that I'll be.

ELFRIDA.

What would I have? I'd have you be the king.
Promotions, dignities, and worthiness

To scatter or withhold, as pleaseth thee.
Be thou the king, and not a cockadoo,
That may not crow nor gather up a crumb
Unless his crested rival be away.

King Edgar.

You fill me with your own ambitious mind.
I know not how to do it. Dunstan holds
So strong a grip upon the sounding chords,
They make no music when I twang the strings.

Elfrida.

Rap on his knuckles with your sceptre till
He gives the harp to you. Thou art the king,
He subject; teach him that, and let him squirm.
"Good-morrow, madam." God defend the king
When none do say, "Long live Your Majesty!"

King Edgar.

He hath advantage in this craft. His years
Have borne so long the burdens of the state,
That I am lost, and cannot find my way.

Elfrida.

No way? No way? I'll set you on the way.
Appoint a day when we shall take our crowns.

Assume the long-forgotten faculties
Amidst such show of pageants, carnivals,
As shall the world set staring for a year;
Create new dignitaries, banish some,
And if sedition lift its dangerous head,
Strike off the head as soon as it doth rise.

King Edgar.

Why, what care I for idle festivals?
Eight kings once drew my barge upon the Thames,
And did me homage. That was Dunstan's care.
Yet I did weigh no more on my return,
Could eat no more, and drink no fuller draughts,
Than if they had but been so many slaves.
'Twill all be one a thousand years from now.

Elfrida.

'Twill not be one a thousand years from now.
Thus Dunstan feeds you on such juicy meat
Before the multitude, yet bids the world
Take note you are his lion, toothless, caged,
And held to draw him profit. In the books
That shall be written when the world is old,
One name shall stand for greatness in this day.
Shall Dunstan live in books and monuments,
Temples and arches, and the songs of maids,—

In memories and blessings, and the pride
Which all the world in human triumph holds,
While some obscure, neglected line shall say,
" 'Tis said there was a king in Dunstan's day."

King Edgar.

It is traditional among our kin
That I was by my good grandmother named.
She might have called me Dunstan, might she not?
How then? And who can tell by what short chance
This bishop 'scaped an Edgaring? The books
And chronicles, the monuments, what not,—
What think you now, Elfrida? Let us say
Henceforth in all the tattling registers
My name is Dunstan. Are you satisfied?
To save my name from dull obscurity,
And keep it pounding at the doors of fame,—
Is that respect which my grandmother's gift
Doth merit? If it die, 'tis safe enough;
But living, what a beggar it may be! [*Exit.*

Elfrida.

So dies my hope that long hath dying been.
O heaven, that I did sell my soul so cheap!
This king, in whom such noble blood doth flow,
Would not so much as raise his hand to strike

The hungry swarm that would devour his state;
But if 'twere threatened to assume his meat,
Or draw one gulp from out his mighty draughts,
He'd murder, kill, and slay, to save his swill.

Enter EDMUND *and* OSRIC.

ELFRIDA.

Right welcome, noble gentlemen.

EDMUND.

Long life befall Your Majesty.

OSRIC.

And happiness to fill your royal breast,
Even as your virtues fill the land with grace.

ELFRIDA.

My lords, I thank you. You have comforted
Full many a time this heavy heart of mine.

EDMUND *and* OSRIC.

'Tis that which honors us.

ELFRIDA.

You oft have seen, and often did lament
The knotted cords which bind our royalty.

If I do put a knife within your hands,
That gives them severance, would you loose one thong,
If it engages not a single fear?

Both.

We would, Your Majesty.

Elfrida.

It is not much I ask. To counsel me
What strength is with the day dissatisfied;
Who partisans of Dunstan, who of us.
And there be many who, a little urged,
Would wake if they could know a leader's plume
Waited their following.

Osric.

You honor us, Your Majesty, you do;
And fear not but we shall be circumspect.
We take our leave with loyal ardor burning,
Our own approval, and Your Grace's earning.

       [*Exeunt.*

Elfrida.

To coward fingers I intrust the brand;
But, let them drop it where they will, it burns,

And shall inflame the kingdom, and engulf
In waves of fire proud Dunstan and his power.

[*Exit.*

Re-enter EDMUND *and* OSRIC.

EDMUND.

Where is Her Majesty?

OSRIC.

I cannot tell.　But now we left her here.

EDMUND.

No matter.　Thou art spokesman for us both.
The slippery, soft, insinuating tongue
Is thine, and from the wary earl of Mercia——

OSRIC.

No　thou shalt open first, and I, being near,
Will watch thy thought's legs, keeping straight the toes
Toward our considered and approved purpose.

EDMUND.

Nay, Osric, see thou dost proceed in this
As something newly thought, a fresh resolve

That is not yet resolved, but labors still
To free itself from many tanglements.
And while the body of our purposes
Is through the earl's allegiance panting up,
I'll say, "Why so I think, my noble earl,
Since Osric brings it forth. What say you to it?"

Enter an OFFICER.

OFFICER.

I have the bishop's warrant for you both,
That with high treason to the king and him
Doth charge you, as shall instantly be shown.
Edmund of Wilton, Osric, lord of Dale,
I here arrest you.

EDMUND.

Arrest us! What's the charge?

OFFICER.

High treason 'gainst His Majesty the king.

OSRIC.

The charge is false! This is a foolish jest.
If I have sinned, 'tis as his partisan.

EDMUND.

Why, what a fright your jest did work in me!

OFFICER.

Here is the warrant, here the signature,
The ink not dry. I guard you to His Grace.

SCENE V.—THE PALACE.

DUNSTAN, EDMUND, OSRIC, *and* ATTENDANTS.

DUNSTAN.

Edmund of Wilton, Osric, lord of Dale,
High treason stands recorded 'gainst your fame;
That each with others acting out the word,
You have contrived against the peace and weal
Of Edgar, his archbishop, and the realm,
In that, by sundry words and promises
To one Elfrida, queen of England, made,
You did engage to kill Lord Dunstan, now
Archbishop of the see of Canterbury.
And, furthermore, to stir sedition up,
And turn against the bishop and the king

All forces and all strength at your control.
How do you answer?

EDMUND.

My lord, 'gainst every word which so is charged
I back my firm denial, sparing Your Grace.

DUNSTAN.

Denial's no defence.

EDMUND.

I beg Your Grace, let truth be my defence.

OSRIC.

No shape nor shadow like the thing declared,
Nor anything that malice might construe
To be so like it, can be chargeable
Against my fair account. Where we have erred
It was in honor of His Majesty.
Against yourself we planned no evil thing——

DUNSTAN.

We charge you, go not to your last account
With that base lie upon your traitor lips.
Take them away. At sunrise let them die,

And all conspiring 'gainst the king, or me,
In whom the king inseparably is lodged,
Take note how hidden things are not concealed.
Lead them away.

>OSRIC.
>
>Hear me again, my lord.

>DUNSTAN.

No more.   [*Exeunt.*
This was the greatest danger to my state,
And dangerously have I met it, too.
Elfrida, I have caged the lioness.

SCENE VI.—A DUNGEON.

EDMUND *and* OSRIC, *and an* OFFICER *without, on guard.*

>EDMUND.

I watched the bishop's eye, alas! Well, I shall sleep the better to-night for it, and not toss and sweat, hoping for a pardon.

SCENE VI.] *Elfrida.* 115

OSRIC.

I pray God I do not dream I am being executed. Let us not sleep. They kill us at sunrise, did he say?

EDMUND.

At sunrise; but 'tis too early. My mind will not come to it till an hour later. Why, look you, I do not know a time I did not wake and stretch my limbs, and sort my dreams from what I did. Woe me! to-morrow, when the air is cold, and I bewildered 'twixt my dreams and fears, shivering, unready, to be hustled off!

OSRIC.

To think of marriage-feasts and merriment,
And no one grieved because I do not come!
New enterprises that shall set the world
In discourse of their wonders, and I dead!
New things, old projects to completeness turned,
And none to bring me word, and none to ask·
While I, imprisoned, tied against redress,
Another boldly to usurp my wife
And in the great world's well-approving eye
To say of Osric's wife, "She is my own."
But no; she could not do it, yet she would.
Such is the manner of the world, alack!
That these adulteries are held no sin,

Because, forsooth, there's never fear nor dread
That any shall come back and find her false.
And this is virtue, this fidelity,
If husbands know not of their wives' offence !

EDMUND.

Ill must we fare to-morrow : ill indeed,
With the dumb spirit mourning o'er the clay,
The horrible eyes that look and cannot see,—
Oh, save me, Osric, for the love of God !

OSRIC.

Alas, alas ! I know not mine offence.
'Tis inconsistent as a morning dream.
Why, what if this were but a frightful dream ?
For I have been as heavy in my sleep,
Bound as inextricably, and awoke,
Or thought I did, if now I am awake,—
If ever I have been awake,—Edmund !

EDMUND.

What's this ? 'Tis more unlikely than a dream.
Now I will nip you ; feel you that, my lord ?
Good faith, good Osric, when I wake again

I'll ask you how you slept, and tell my fright.
"If ever I have been awake!"
Why, so the dream goes on, to-morrow comes,
Chops me my head off, which they toss about;
Then down I lie, and dream it on again.
So has it been with legs, why not with heads?
When I awake I'll find myself in bed,
Spreading my arms, and reaching at the air,
Or under it, perchance——
                    How thick my brain!
I would the dream were over, if I dream!

OFFICER.

We contradict oblivion at our birth,
And through a span of incongruities
Piece out a congruous day; and then comes death,
The flat and final contradiction
Of this loud assertive life. Pass on, swift hours,
While laughter, which doth serve persistent hope,
Stands arguing with despair when hope is gone.
Poor fools! I grudge ye not your merriment.

EDMUND.

There is a heaviness upon my eyes,
As if they sulked to see the blessed sun.

Osric.

What? (*Sleeps.*)

Edmund.

She gave——to-morrow——ho! (*Sleeps.*

SCENE VII.—THE PALACE.

King Edgar *and* Elfrida.

Elfrida.

My lord——

King Edgar.

Nay, do not speak to me. I know thy thought.

Elfrida.

I will, I must speak out with all my strength.
If thou didst ever love me, or do now,
Let not this shame to me, this wrong to those
Who were my coaxed adherents, so be done.
They are as guiltless of another fault
As one unborn, but that I did engage

For you and in the welfare of us all,
That they should counsel me who were my friends,
And who my foes.

King Edgar.

Away, thou meddling she!

Elfrida.

And doth Elfrida's friendship merit death?
Oh, foul, besotted beast! that lets this shame
Attend thy queen. I am a stagnant pool,
Breathing a noxious, fetid vapor forth,
Stared at and pointed out by travellers,
Who on the distant heights do hold the nose!

King Edgar.

Be what thou wilt, my lady. Clothe thy name
In such comparisons as pleaseth thee.

Elfrida.

Oh, I, that might have been the very fount
Of benefits, am sealed and stocked with toads,
Green slimy frogs, foul things, and poisonous weeds.
Dead things do rot upon me, and a wreck
That once with white sails did convey my hope!

King Edgar.

'Tis not a pleasing picture; no, 'tis not.

Elfrida.

Thy slavish, brutish self hath made it true.
No man shall ever look on me again
But in contempt and loathing. None shall dare
To better my estate, but he must die.
Oh, Edgar, canst thou see me brought so low,
And think I am thy true and chosen queen?

King Edgar.

None but thyself should use such words of thee.
If that be comfort, take it to thy heart.

Elfrida.

None but myself may show my portrait up,
Yet Dunstan may two adherents kill
For naught but that they were my partisans.

King Edgar.

Be still. While Dunstan lets me have my way,
I yours, there's naught but folly left to say.

ELFRIDA.

So Dunstan lets you! Now thou slave, farewell.
A lion caged to-day I said thou art,—
A swine art thou that wallows in the mire,
Grunting his thanks to Dunstan for his life.

ACT V

SCENE I.—THE PALACE.

ATHELWOLD, *disguised as* KENNETH.

ATHELWOLD.

How weak and pale from wounds and grief I am!
There was an Athelwold that paced these halls,
And found no griefs in all his bounded life
Save those he conjured from their dark abode.
He was an Athelwold who well devised
Full many a cunning plan to check the ills
Of others sorrowing. Now walks he here
Beside his uninvited miseries,
And all his " this, or haply that I'd do,
If so it be that this should come to him,"
Serves every purpose but accomplishment.
Now, if she had not wedded with the king!
But 'tis my triumph to have brought her low
In these disguises. Kenneth she doth love,

But she would give her soul if Athelwold
Might never know of it. Ha, ha!

Enter ELFRIDA.

ELFRIDA.

My lord,
May I not join your laughter?

ATHELWOLD.

No, my love,
For 'tis the saddest thing in all the world
Provokes my mirth.

ELFRIDA.

How strange that this can be!

ATHELWOLD.

The tailor laughs to see a tattered coat,
The seller's gain feeds on the buyer's loss,
The starling's sorrow is the eagle's mirth,
And death begets all heirs. The joy of one
Is ever planted in his fellow's grief,
And thus the saddest thing in all the world
Provokes the gayest laughter. Thou wouldst weep

To know my merriment; so ask me not.
Shall I not take my leave?

    ELFRIDA.
       Your leave, my lord?

    ATHELWOLD.
Farewell, Elfrida.

    ELFRIDA.
     Canst thou say farewell,
When that farewell doth make me fare so ill?
Oh, Kenneth, there is benediction hid
In every word of thine, save only that
Which most should carry it.

    ATHELWOLD.
       You love the king.

    ELFRIDA.
I hate him, for he loves me like a beast,
And from my arms I long have banished him.

    ATHELWOLD.
Since thou art faithless to thy chosen liege,
So thou wilt be to me. Elfrida, hark:

This is not lover's language. Look not so.
Thou hadst a husband once whom thou didst love;
What was his name?

ELFRIDA.

I dare not speak his name.

ATHELWOLD.

Then let it be unspoken. He is dead.
Is it not true, my lady, he is dead?

ELFRIDA.

Oh, Kenneth, thou dost break a bruised reed.
His name was Athelwold, and he is dead.

ATHELWOLD.

True, Athelwold is dead. Now let us say
That he doth linger still among the quick.
Once thou didst measure all thy life by him,
And queried if a ribbon or a gem
Would please him better worn this way or that;
And shame had made his bed upon thy cheek,
And forced hot tear-drops from thy sleepless eyes,
If he had known thee listless in the care
Of so slight fancies. Now we'll say he lives,

And thou art measured still by his regard,
How wouldst thou stand in thine own estimate
If he could see thee as thou art this day?

ELFRIDA.

Oh, would that I were buried and at peace!
Eternal silence should lie down with me,
And none interrogate, with hope to gain
A shameful answer from my stubborn lips.

ATHELWOLD.

So thou dost see thyself through Athelwold,
And as thou seest thyself my fears do show.
But I can love thee anywhere but here,
Where, scorched with jealousy, my heart burns up,
And turns to bitterness. Then fly with me.
If thou dost love me, let the booming waves
Beat as they may, we'll stand the rudest shocks.

ELFRIDA.

Thou seest I am weeping. Speak for me.

ATHELWOLD.

Elfrida, words are made of idle air.
The wind that fills a sail bulged toward a port

Inviting thrift and courage, tells a tale
That hissing, sputtering words could never speak.

Enter PHILIP, *who passes.*

PHILIP.

If there be no roguery in this, then is the truth a fable, and wisdom a trap into which many fall. But the king doth not know of it, so he is content; and I know of it, but 'tis naught to me, and they know it who are most delighted. Egad, I know not who are happiest, those who know or those who are in ignorance. I have seen the same with them ere this day. But 'tis none of my jubilee, and I'm off. [*Exit.*

ATHELWOLD.

Elfrida, do not go. He's but a clown.
[*Exit* ELFRIDA.
My love makes peace between contempt and love;
If I shall kill them, or she flies with me,
I care not which. Nay, I shall kill the king,
And spare her for rehearsal of my wrongs.
No flattery is more soothing than the tears
Of one who hath inflicted hopeless grief.
[*Exit.*

PHILIP *and* SANCIE *below.* ELFRIDA *passes.*

SANCIE.

Lord, did you see Her Majesty's face when she passed that door? The devil hath strangled her good angel, and I know it.

PHILIP.

Woman, for a woman who knows nothing, you know too much.

SANCIE.

Lord, Philip, you're too much for me; but if I know nothing, how can I know too much?

PHILIP.

You know all that you never learned. That's everything, and too much for anybody to know.

SANCIE.

Ee-he! you're too much for me. But the devil hath gibbered at her pillow, poor soul! [*Exeunt.*

SCENE II.—THE PALACE.

Roxie *and* Philip.

Roxie.

Philip, thou art indeed a noble youth,
Valiant as strong, and strong as Hercules.
I never knew how well the lion hid
Beneath that outward gentle coat of thine
Till your own lips did mind me of his lair.

Philip.

Oh, say you so, and think it as you say?

Roxie.

Nay, sniffle not; be brave when ladies' praise
Comes floating daintily on perfumed breath,
As when the hurricane of peril yells
Rough but dear music in thy fearless ear.

Philip.

Well, so I am a trifle boldly made,
Heroically built, egad, and tall;

But not too tall; oh, no; enough.
Ah, Roxie, things must come when I go for 'em.
But no philosopher; oh, no; no sage,
But witty? Gad! Roxie, my humor's off,
But you have heard me when my tongue is loose,
And it is scissors. These adapted things,
Which seem as they were studied in the night——

Roxie.

Yes, now, Philip, that's a good fellow.

Philip.

With beetles, bats, and stinging things to teach——

Roxie.

Yes, now, Philip——

Philip.

Nay, let me finish up.
They come while yet premeditation sits
In desperation, looking for his wits.
And there it goes again, as easily
As one can stretch his mouth and say "Heigho!"
It was my mother's gift.

Roxie.

                Oh, blessed soul,
That had so kind and lovable a son!
Now, Philip, I have left my harp long stand
Upon the stairway, sadly out of tune;
I pray you fetch it down again to me.
                [*Exit* Philip.
This praise would pay his charges to the moon.
Oh, I can spend a minute merrily
To hear him tell what kind of man he is,—
But not two minutes. 'Tis to-day his wit,
To-morrow valor and a bloody soul;
The next day tenderness, humility,
Or haply wrath, or haply anything
As he may see a pattern pleasing him,
Which his miscomprehension may impair.

        Re-enter Philip.

Thanks. Philip; you're an angel.

Philip.

Ah, no indeed, you do not know me yet;
Too much of Adam——

ROXIE.

Oh, I see, I see.
No angel, but a man of heavier grain.

PHILIP.

That's it.

ROXIE.

But too much given, I think, to idle boasts
That do not take their warrant from your deeds.

PHILIP.

Eh! Gad, not a bit of it!

ROXIE.

Philip, I fear it is more truth than none.

PHILIP.

Why, hear you, Roxie. Though I seem to boast,
I do not tell the half that I have done.
If one should say, I passed me through the hall,
Met no one, and did seat me on a chair,
Said nothing, and did make no person stare,
This in another man would be no boast,
Whose word bears just proportion to his deed.

Roxie.

Oh, Philip, thou art incorrigible.

Philip.

And invincible.   Now hear you——

Roxie.

Nay, call it so.   I know not what you'd say,
But rather far than hear the thing declared,
I will admit it.   Where's Lord Kenneth now?

Philip.

Consorting with the queen, I'll wager heads.
That goes without the saying.   Find the queen——

Roxie.

You wrong Her Majesty, you know you do.
She is the sweetest soul that draws a breath;
And though in me, or any less than she,
This friendship for my lord were indiscreet——

Philip.

Indiscreet!   Yes, that is a good word.   One may say that before ladies, and it means the same as the other.   Here comes Her Majesty.

Enter ELFRIDA.

ELFRIDA.

Philip, I give you leave to go.   [*Exit* PHILIP.
Why keep you this ill-mannered clown about,
Who smirks and looks askance, then drops his eyes,
Then lifts them up to hunt for comets' tails,
As if he were the fount, the rill, the river,
And the huge sea in which all knowledge flows?

ROXIE.

It is a trick he hath of late assumed,
But who did teach it him is past my wit.

ELFRIDA.

What said he on my coming?

ROXIE.

"Here comes Her Majesty."

ELFRIDA.

Before that did he say nothing?

ROXIE.

Why, I did twit him on his boasting some,
And buoy him up with open flatteries.

ELFRIDA.

He lies, I say! Have you not heard him lie?

ROXIE.

Oh, dear, yes.

ELFRIDA.

And if he wags that idle tongue of his
To my disparagement, God rest his soul!
I'll send it to him. Said he aught of me?

ROXIE.

He would not come to me to sell his smut.

ELFRIDA.

Nor nowhere. Roxie, I am very sad.
Pray leave me here alone. Forgive me, though:
If I could rule the chances of this world,
You would have been my mother's blessed child.
Thou art to Roger what I once have been
Unto another. Searching all the world,
Was none so happy, innocent as I,
Until—no matter.

ROXIE.

Oh, my sweet sister, since you wish me so,
May I not help you through this wilderness,
Where much I fear your feet are tangled up
'Mongst intricate and tortuous ways?

ELFRIDA.

No, leave me. [*Exit* ROXIE.
If he doth tell the little he did see,
And image his surmises to the king,
I will not see Lord Kenneth more alone,
Though he should coax and tease as lover-like
As—Kenneth. Is it sin I love him so?
Then God forgive me, trampling on his gift!
Roxie!

Enter ATHELWOLD, *disguised as* KENNETH.

Oh, Kenneth, leave me!

ATHELWOLD.

No, love, I will not leave you in this world.
When mutual vows and holy promises
Do for a fuller consummation wait
Upon the benediction of the Powers,
That graciously did witness what was vowed.

The year may skimp four seasons to a day,
For heedless love doth scorn the calendar.
But when 'tis irritated, goaded, plagued,
Scotched with the lash of such a rivalry,
It will not wait even on necessity.

ELFRIDA.

I do implore you, leave me to myself.

ATHELWOLD.

I am yourself, and you are none but me.
I know a haven in a port remote
Where love may fold its wings and sing all day,
And none would guess those wings had ever fanned
The hot exhalements from the devil's face.

ELFRIDA.

Oh, treason, Kenneth! pray you say no more.

ATHELWOLD.

I cannot choose my words; they fall like rain.
But of this habit, which conceals me now,
I shall divest my coward self, and stand
Within the hour the person that I am.
I have a history. It pleaseth me
To show what knocks and bruises scar my soul,

Got on this bouncing, jolting course of life.
Come with me on this little portico.

ELFRIDA.

Oh, Kenneth!

ATHELWOLD.

What is it?

ELFRIDA.

                I fear the night.

ATHELWOLD.

The night hath fled before these lights, as fly
Unhallowed spirits at the name of Christ.

ELFRIDA.

But this forbidden concord of our hearts——

ATHELWOLD.

And who forbids?

ELFRIDA.

The king, the law, high heaven, and the world.

ATHELWOLD.

And who invites?

ELFRIDA.

Thou, Kenneth, who art more than king and law,
Dearer than heaven.

ATHELWOLD.

How still the air! How silently the Night
Holds its mistrusted rein, while jealous Day
Guards with a thousand eyes the quiet earth,
O'er which the ominous queen is brooding!
See how the moon comes up with modest blush,
As when she bent to print upon the cheek
Of the fair shepherd her first amorous kiss,
Yet comes so royally that baffled Night
Hides in the deep recess of wood and glen.
The drowsy flowers half ope their dewy eyes,
And, wondering if 'tis day, fall back again,
To dream of dalliance with the butterflies.
Knowest thou this hand?

ELFRIDA.

Why, Kenneth!

ATHELWOLD.

What now?

ELFRIDA.

Why, I do know this hand; indeed I do.

ATHELWOLD.

I tell thee, love, it is not safe, not safe.
The king, methinks, hath nearly winded us.
To-night, into this distant haven borne,
Our love must find a refuge.   'Tis not safe.

ELFRIDA.

Oh, Kenneth, love, I dare not thus desert.
The realm would heave and shake in every part,
And cast us back upon that purple wrath,
Which fears not God nor pities any man.
I beg, I do implore you, leave me now.

ATHELWOLD.

You never loved me.

ELFRIDA.

Now hear if I do not.   Depart at once.
Put off these garments that now cover you,
And in another guise return again.

ATHELWOLD.

Why, so I shall; and thou shalt see the garb
And strange concealments to deceive the court.
Into this chamber I shall now depart,
And presently return. Prepare your soul,
For I shall fright you when I come again.
  [*Exit* KENNETH, *who immediately returns as*
    ATHELWOLD.

ELFRIDA.

Oh, God!

ATHELWOLD.

Hush!

ELFRIDA.

Oh, do not touch me! Athelwold! Help! help!

ATHELWOLD.

No, calm your spirit, for I am no ghost,
But he whom you thought Kenneth even now.
See how my hands are tangible and warm.

ELFRIDA.

Nay, it is Athelwold that's dead, interred,
Wandering to right some wrong that hath been done.

ATHELWOLD.

I say 'tis Kenneth; Athelwold is dead,
For Edgar killed him when he took his love.
But Edgar's spear, less cruel than thou art,
Did make a wound too fleeting for his care.
Yes, Athelwold is dead, his heart is dead,
But 'twas inconstancy that gave the blow.

ELFRIDA.

Oh, be thou ghost or living, Athelwold,
If thou hast power to avenge thy wrongs,
Wreak out thy bloody vengeance and depart,
Leaving no index to my book of shame.
Eternal hell should compensate this crime,
And leave my name unscathed by envious time.

ATHELWOLD.

I am no ghost, but I am Athelwold,
A frame inanimate, borne by a dream
Amidst the vaporing splendors of the world
To seek its errant soul. I found it here.

Enter KING EDGAR.

King Edgar.

I'll send that soul to heaven presently.
Elfrida, get you gone, false brimming queen,
Who turns the palace to a bordel-house,
And wanders browsing through the shameless night
With every prowling beast that bellows love!

Elfrida.

Oh, my liege——

King Edgar.

Out, spunky queen!

[*Exit* Elfrida.

Now, thou that searchest for thy errant soul——
Oh, gracious God!

Athelwold.

Ay, Edgar, thou hast need to call on God,
For thou this night shalt see him.

King Edgar.

What art thou?

Athelwold.

A man, my lord; my name is Athelwold.

King Edgar.

Why, I did kill thee, and thy flesh was torn
From off thy supple limbs by birds and beasts,
And thy still bones were decently interred.

Athelwold.

Ay, thou didst kill me, Edgar; true, 'tis true.
And now that boon shall I perform for you.
    [Edgar *retreats slowly backward.* Athelwold
        follows. Edgar *stops.*

King Edgar.

Now, spirit, this unseemly chase is spent,
And I, who did destroy thy mortal part,
Here challenge thy perpetual soul, the league,
Confederated fiends in thy behalf,
And all the agencies of fiery hell,
This all unequal contest I assume;
But when my spirit is as free as thine,
Hate to thy hate, down-tumbling through the gulf,
Clutching and clawing, we shall have it out.

Athelwold.

This sword is steel, and not a shadowy blade;
This arm is flesh, and not a fleeting shade.

KING EDGAR.

Thou lying vapor!

ATHELWOLD.

Down, down, thou murderous hulk!
(*They fight. Both fall.*)
I, that was Kenneth, now am Athelwold,
But shall be neither ere the moment pass.
It was a mortal wound thou gavest me,
And mortally have I avenged the blow.   (*Dies.*)

KING EDGAR.

Wait, coward Athelwold, till I can die;
But thou shalt not escape, fly as thou wilt.
(*Dies.*)

Re-enter ELFRIDA.

ELFRIDA.

Oh Athelwold, my love, my love, come back!
I will not let thee die!   One other word,
To say I did not seek thy life, my love,

Nor wrong thee wittingly.   Foul, foul and false
Hath mad ambition made me, and my prayer
Comes echoing back from the shut gates of heaven,
And all is over save my tears and shame.

THE END.